To the Warriors.

Designed by Marilyn F. Appleby.
Edited by Kathleen D. Valenzi, with the assistance of Ross A. Howell Jr.,
Gina M. Wallace, and Carlotta M. Eike.

Library of Congress Catalog Card Number 87-81300
ISBN 0-943231-00-0
Printed and bound in Japan by Dai Nippon Printing Co., Ltd.
Published by Howell Press, Inc., 2000 Holiday Drive,
Charlottesville, Virginia 22901. Telephone (804) 977-4006.
First Edition

HOWELL PRESS

FORGED IN STEEL

U.S. MARINE CORPS AVIATION

PHOTOGRAPHY BY C.J. HEATLEY III

INTRODUCTION BY SENATOR JOHN GLENN

FORGED IN STEEL

The year 1987 marks the 75th anniversary of Marine Corps aviation. This book is a tribute to that legacy.

These first 75 years of Marine Corps Aviation have spanned the history of military aviation, from its infancy in rudimentary flying machines to today's highly sophisticated space-age technology. A review of the three-quarters of a century underscores the Corps' proud aviation heritage, a heritage in which I was privileged to play an active part for well over two decades.

From its founding in 1912, Marine Corps aviation has been noted for its close coordination with the other services, particularly the Navy, with which the Marine Corps serves as an equal military service in the Department of the Navy. From its inception Marine Corps aviation has had as its primary focus the support of Marine ground forces. Though Marine Corps aviation personnel are sometimes loath to acknowledge it, Marine aviation has always been primarily a supporting arm for the infantry trooper on the ground. In fulfilling this role, Marine Corps aviation over the years has evolved into a full-spectrum force of tactical aviation, including fighter, attack, reconnaissance, helicopter, transport, and air-control elements, an active and reserve force today consisting of well over 1,300 aircraft and manned by approximately one-quarter of the Marine Corps' 243,000 personnel.

I'm sure such impressive latter-day capabilities were scarcely imagined by First Lieutenant Alfred A. Cunningham, U.S. Marine Corps, when, on May 22, 1912, he reported for duty at the new aviation camp in Annapolis, Maryland. On August 1 of that same year, after two hours and 40 minutes of instruction at Marblehead, Massachusetts, Lieutenant Cunningham soloed in a Curtiss seaplane, thereby qualifying to become the Marine Corps' first pilot. Thus was born Marine Corps aviation, destined to become a vital element both of the Marine Corps and of America's military strength.

In 1917, just five short years after its birth, Marine Corps aviation, like other elements of the U.S. military, started to expand rapidly as America geared up for entry into World War I. From the outset, the Corps was assigned two disparate aviation missions—reflecting its close relationship with the Navy, while still emphasizing direct support of Marines—antisubmarine patrol using seaplanes, and ground support using landplanes. Notably, the Marines' 1st Aeronautic Company (seaplanes), became the first fully trained and equipped American aviation unit to go overseas in World War I when it was dispatched to the Azores in early 1918 to fly antisubmarine patrols.

By the end of the war, the First Marine Aviation Force, based in France, had flown fighter and ground-support missions, both with the RAF and on its own, in support of Marine Corps and Allied forces. In air-to-air combat, Marine flight crews had shot down four German fighters, and had claimed eight more; four Marine flight-crew members had been killed in action in those engagements. By the armistice, Marine aviation had expanded to 282 officers, 2,180 enlisted Marines, and 340 aircraft.

As a consequence of demobilization after World War I, Marine aviation, like the forces of all the military services, experienced a significant reduction in both personnel and equipment. Even so, innovative Marine Corps development in air-ground operations, initiated in France in 1918, was aggressively continued by the Corps in the years following the armistice. Those early attempts at close coordination between aviation and ground forces were to be the springboard for building the highly effective Marine Corps air/ground team concept of operations which has become the hallmark of today's Marine Corps.

During the period between World War I and World War II, Marine aviation saw expeditionary duty in a variety of missions, including working with the government to put down bandits in Haiti in 1919. Later, during the Second Nicaraguan Intervention in 1927, Marine aviation was detailed to assist the Nicaraguan government in suppressing guerrilla forces. In Nicaragua, the Marines conducted what was probably the first organized dive-bombing attack in history, and further honed air-ground coordination skills with Marine pilots acting as observers for ground forces. Given the success of Marine aviation in Central America, the United States opted to deploy expeditionary forces containing similar air detachments to China and the Dominican Republic in the ensuing period before World War II.

By the end of the 1930s, the Department of the Navy had clarified the role of Marine Corps aviation. The Corps' new formally defined, primary aviation mission was to organize, equip, and train Marine Corps aviation elements for support of the Fleet Marine Force both in landing operations and in the field, and to act as replacements for Navy carrier-based units when directed. This re-defined mission served the Corps well in preparing it for the severe challenges it was to face in the cauldron of World War II.

I was a 20-year-old college student when the Japanese attacked Pearl Harbor on December 7, 1941, and, like many Americans, I joined up immediately for active military duty. Because I already had my private pilot's license and loved to fly, I enlisted in the Navy as an Aviation Cadet. Shortly after enlisting, I was sent to Corpus Christi, Texas, for military pilot-training, where I received my wings as a Naval Aviator a year later.

My Marine Corps career got its start inadvertently one day during flight training when my best friend, Tom Miller, and I returned to our barracks to find a notice posted on the bulletin board listing the names of pilots with sufficiently high grades in both ground school and flight training to be qualified to apply for a commission in the Marine Corps. All those who were interested were directed to report to the cadet recreation center that afternoon for the Marine Corps brief on a career with the Leathernecks. Since Tom and I were both on the list, we decided to attend the meeting.

As we walked in, a bit late, a young Marine captain, already an air-combat veteran of the early action in the South Pacific, was delivering the standard service sales-pitch. He told all of us that if we wanted to be the best, we should join the Marines. I was a bit skeptical. Then the captain issued a challenge: "We don't think you're good enough to be one of us." Who could resist that? We both signed up immediately. The more than 23 years that I would eventually serve in Marine Corps aviation were the most stimulating and fulfilling of my life. (My close friend Tom Miller would go on to have a truly distinguished Marine Corps career in three wars; after 37 years on active duty, Tom retired in 1979 as a Lieutenant General and head of Marine Corps aviation.)

My first taste of operational military flying was in the Navy PBY flying boat — a large, lumbering, multi-engine seaplane primarily used as a reconnaissance and antisubmarine platform. Flying PBYs might seem a little odd for someone who wanted to be a Marine Corps fighter pilot. But the bootleg word in Corpus was that the Marine Corps was getting the hot P-38 Lockheed Lighting, and that preference for assignment to Marine Corps P-38 squadrons would go to those with multi-engine time.

Consequently, after a bit of wangling I succeeded in getting assigned to advanced training in the PBYs, gaining gunnery and navigation experience as I bounced around Corpus Christi Bay and the Gulf of Mexico. When there was a submarine alert, we cadets frequently would be hauled out of bed in the middle of the night to search for German U-boats in the Gulf. The presence of thousands of tons of Allied shipping on the bottom of the Gulf attests to the effectiveness of German U-Boat actions there during the war, however, I never once saw a German submarine in all of my many hours of peering at the Gulf, aching to be a part of a live attack on an enemy sub and to "get into the war." (While I did get my multi-engine time, it was to little avail in my getting into a P-38 squadron, since Marine Corps procurement of that excellent fighter turned out to be nothing more than rumor.)

For Marine Corps aviation, World War II was an all-up, all-out effort. The Japanese had dealt the American military a devastating blow with their strike at Pearl Harbor and their heavy attacks that immediately followed throughout the Pacific. By the summer of 1942, however, the United States was rapidly overcoming the most serious damage to American military capabilities in the Theater.

On August 7, 1942, the Marine Corps landed on Tulagi and on the adjacent, larger island of Guadalcanal. One of the Corps' first objectives was to capture the partially completed Japanese airfield on "the Canal" to provide an ashore operating base for Marine Air coming off the carriers. After heavy fighting the airfield was taken, and the Marine Corps commenced air operations almost immediately. They named the strip Henderson Field in honor of Major Lofton R. Henderson, a Marine dive-bomber pilot who had been shot down at the battle of Midway two months before. The Guadalcanal campaign, though ultimately successful, became a lesson in perseverance for the Corps, as appalling shortages of virtually all supplies earned their desperate battle to retain and expand their toehold on the island the name "Operation Shoestring."

But in that first of the Pacific Island campaigns, Marines fighter pilots, based at Henderson Field and flying primarily F4F Wildcats, shattered the myth that Japanese pilots and

their Zero fighters were invincible, inflicting heavy losses on the enemy in the air as the Marine Corps consolidated its hold on the island. In February 1943, a new Marine fighter, the Chance-Vought F4U arrived at Guadalcanal; it was faster, had more firepower, and had twice the range of any Japanese fighter. This was the famed "Corsair," that gull-winged beautiful flying machine that even today springs to mind first when thinking of Marine Corps aviation. By the middle of 1943, all eight Marine fighter squadrons in the South Pacific were flying that superb aircraft, an aircraft that I was destined to fly for more hours than any other during my time in the Corps.

In 1943 it became clear that we were winning the war in the Pacific but at a horrifying cost in human life in places like Tarawa and Kwajalein, where Marine pilots were based in order to assault the bypassed Marshall atolls in what came to be known, in a classic misnomer, as "milk runs." The stench of death filled the air on these islands long after we stormed the beaches.

In the summer of 1943, the American fleet's actions in the Coral Sea and at Midway halted the Japanese advance, and America prepared to take the offensive throughout the Theater. However, heavy American losses, among other factors, prompted a U.S. decision to bypass the other atolls in the Marshalls. Instead, we decided to neutralize the Japanese-held islands by massive bombing. In support of that effort my squadron was catapulted off the deck of a carrier to land at Majuro atoll. It was at Majuro that I flew my first combat mission in March 1944, and it was there that the war became very personal when my wingman and close friend Monte

Goodman was hit by anti-aircraft fire and became our first squadron-member killed in action.

After the successful American campaign at Guadalcanal, Marine Corps aviation supported a series of island-hopping campaigns throughout the Pacific. However, until 1944 Marine aviators in the Central Pacific had been largely limited to flying land-based missions, since the Navy was reluctant to provide the escort carriers from which the Marines could fly.

But in 1944 two factors forced the decision to put Marine squadrons aboard carriers. First, the enormous distances between objectives in the Central Pacific mandated that Marine squadrons be based afloat in order to be able to support Marine ground forces on the beach prior to their moving air ashore once an airstrip was taken. Secondly, the heavy Navy aviation losses caused by the newly initiated Japanese kamikaze raids necessitated the employment of Marine fighter squadrons to increase the fighter strength of the large, fast carriers.

The last great battle of World War II was fought on and around Okinawa from April to June of 1945. During the campaign, Marine Corps aviation supported the Army and the Navy, as well as Marine forces, day and night. Operating both from aircraft carriers and from land bases, Marine flyers employed with great effectiveness the close-air-support tactics that had been so hard learned throughout the war. Indeed, it had been said of this support somewhat earlier in the war that the only way to employ it closer and more effectively was to put bayonets on the wing tips.

Shortly after World War II, rotary-wing aviation burst onto the scene; almost immediately it became obvious that the helicopter would have a profound impact on the roles and missions of Marine aviation, especially in amphibious warfare. The need for wider tactical dispersion dictated by the advent of atomic weapons led the Marine Corps to develop the concept of vertical envelopment, which employed helicopters to bypass enemy strong points, thus creating a whole new capability in offensive operations.

During the Korean War from 1950 to 1953, Marine Corps aviation skillfully blended the new with the old. Helicopters and jets were used alongside old reliables such as the Corsair in supporting Marine ground forces. Put to the test, the helicopter quickly proved its value, and emerged as one of the Korean War's most significant new weapons. In addition to reconnaissance, troop transport, and aerial re-supply, Marine helicopters conducted nearly 10,000 medical evacuations during the war and, on occasion, even functioned as rudimentary weapon platforms, presaging the development of helicopter gunships later in the decade.

In Korea, I was fortunate to be able to fly jet-attack missions in the Marine Corps F9F

Panther, as we provided close-air support for our Marines and other friendlies on the ground, as well as flying interdiction strikes deep into North Korea to hit such targets as truck convoys, trains and rail yards, and bridges. But I also wanted to get in the fighter war in air-to-air combat with the North Korean MIGs. However, the Air Force had the primary land-based, air-superiority mission, so Marine aviators had little chance to get in that arena.

When, close to the end of the war, an opportunity arose to volunteer to fly F-86 Sabre jets with the Air Force as an exchange pilot, I jumped at the chance. Before the war ended in July 1953 I had three MIG kills to my credit, while champing at the bit to get two more to achieve standing as a fighter ace. But it had been a hard-fought war. The United States and its United Nations allies had taken a lot of casualties in courageously preventing the Communists from taking over South Korea, and the war could not have ended a day too soon for those of us involved.

After I returned to the United States I successfully applied for Navy test-pilot training at Patuxent River. Once fully qualified I was involved in a number of flight-test programs, but perhaps none as satisfying as my work with the Chance-Vought F8U Crusader, an aircraft that was to deliver yeoman service to the Marine Corps and the Navy before it was retired from active service many years later.

One of the more exciting events in my work with the Crusader was my record-setting flight in 1957 from NAS Los Alamitos, California, to NAS Floyd Bennett, New York, when, for the first time, an aircraft was flown across the continental United States at an average speed greater than Mach 1, the speed of sound. We termed the mission "Operation Bullet," because the aircraft average cross-country speed was faster than the muzzle velocity of a round fired from a service .45 caliber automatic. The Crusader was a great performer, and remains in my heart today second only to the Corsair.

In early 1959 I, along with three Navy pilots and three Air Force pilots, was selected as one of our nation's first group of astronauts. Our assignment was Project Mercury, a mission to prove that the United States could put a man into space and that he could function productively there. For me the culmination of Project Mercury came on February 20, 1962, in my spacecraft "Friendship 7," when I became the first American to orbit the earth. It was an exciting — in fact exhilarating — time. I will always view with pride my involvement in our nation's first major step towards our moon landing some seven years later. Even more, I think of the Mercury program as laying the necessary groundwork for our upcoming space stations and for U.S. manned missions into other parts of our solar system that I trust we will launch by the turn of the century.

After Korea, the Marine Corps put heavier emphasis on improving the battlefield mobility of even larger and better equipped units. By the early 1960s, with the design and procurement of heavy-lift helicopters, Marine infantry and artillery units became largely helicopter-transportable. To capitalize on this new capability, the Marine Corps worked with the Navy to develop amphibious-assault ships as helicopter landing-platforms — ships able to carry both Marine helicopters and troops, and capable of launching sizable vertical-envelopment assaults to objective areas close to coast lines all over the world. (This effort was eminently successful. Today the United States Navy has eleven Amphibious Assault ships in active service. The newer and larger class of these ships also carries surface assault-landing craft in addition to helicopters and troops.)

In April 1962 Marine aviation was again committed to combat, this time in the growing conflict in Southeast Asia. Marine operational involvement in the Vietnam War began when a transport-helicopter squadron was deployed from North Carolina and given the mission of lifting soldiers of the South Vietnamese Army into combat against Communist guerrillas. This small-scale operation, code-named "Shufly," continued until March 1965, when an increase in enemy activity resulted in the landing of a Marine air-ground task force of brigade size some miles south of Da Nang.

Immediately upon landing, the force constructed an airfield at the newly established base of Chu Lai, a Marine Corps airfield which was to become noted for its extremely effective use of the Marine Corps' innovative Short Airfield for Tactical Support (SATS) system. This system employs catapults and arresting gear similar to aircraft carriers, and allows deployment of high-performance, tactical aircraft ashore early in an amphibious operation in an area where no airfield had existed just days before.

In Vietnam, more than any previous war, Marine Corps aviation was able to devote most of its energies to support of Marine "grunts." Marine Corps fixed-wing squadrons, principally flying F-4, A-4, A-6, OV-10, and KC-130 aircraft, were heavily involved in Vietnam from the outset of the initial buildup in 1965 until U.S. withdrawal of most Marine forces in the early 1970s. But Vietnam has been rightly called the helicopter war, because virtually every type of operational Marine Corps helicopter saw service, including the H-34, H-46, H-53, UH-1, and AH-1, in completing troop transport, re-supply, medical evacuation, reconnaissance, and gunship support missions. Together the fixed-wing, helicopter, and air-control elements of Marine aviation compiled a record of combat and combat support second to none.

In the dozen or so years since Vietnam, Marine Corps aviation modernization and doctrinal evolution have continued at a rapid pace, drawing heavily on the lessons learned at the cost of so much blood in Southeast Asia. The very effective F/A-18, A-6E, and AV-8B aircraft are prominent in the fighter and attack units, the OV-10D is the reconnaissance aircraft, and the CH-53E, one of the finest all-around helicopters in the world, leads the way in the rotary-wing inventory along with the UH-1N for command and control, and the new AH-1W as the attack helicopter.

The KC-130T transport and aerial refueler continues to provide an excellent internal logistics capability, both for aerial refueling and for cargo. Lastly, the Marine Air Command and Control System (MACCS) has taken maximum advantage of the recent quantum leaps in electronic technology to update its equipment in order to provide one of the most modern expeditionary air-control capabilities in the world.

Perhaps the greatest shortfall in meeting current Marine Corps aviation needs is in the troop-carrying helicopter, a mission now being handled by the well worn CH-46. Once again the Marine Corps has elected to take the innovative route in selecting the MV-22 Osprey tilt-rotor as the best follow-on aircraft. (This decision is reminiscent of one made almost 20 years ago when the Corps opted to buy the then very controversial AV-8A Harrier vectored-thrust VSTOL attack aircraft to replace the aging A-4.) In procuring the MV-22, the Marine Corps is taking a substantial technical risk in order to achieve a much needed capability for greater mobility and dispersion.

The MV-22, which is due to be in the inventory by 1991, will take off and land like a helicopter and will cruise like a fixed-wing aircraft, giving the Marine Corps dramatically improved assault capability and enhanced survivability in a modern, war-fighting environment. With its improved avionics, greater speed and range, in-flight refueling, and tremendous assault capabilities, the Osprey will add substantially to the flexibility and combat effectiveness of the Marine Corps.

In this abbreviated overview of Marine Corps aviation history we need to underscore several unique elements. Of special significance is Marine aviation's close kinship with Navy aviation. Every Marine Corps aviator is a "Naval Aviator" by formal designation, and the often used term "Navy/Marine Corps team" aptly describes the close relationship of the two services. This close collaboration with the Navy in particular, but also with the other services, has been crucial in honing Marine Corps aviation into the flexible and effective military weapon that it is today.

But of first importance, always, is the Marine Corps' immediate readiness for combat. Indeed, readiness is the key to combat effectiveness. As the Minuteman force of America's defenses, the Marine Corps' dictum "First to Fight," accurately captures its unique role as the nation's ready-force, a force that is prepared at all times to enter combat utilizing all available elements of fighting power under one command. Marines Corps aviation continues to excel as a major element in that capability.

But while cutting-edge technology is crucial to any military endeavor, the human element is paramount. The most important factor in any organization is its people, and Marine aviation is no exception. A nation can have the best equipment in the world; however, that equipment is of but limited value without well-trained, proud, and dedicated men and women to employ it. As General Roy Geiger, one of the most decorated Marines in history and a commander of both ground and air units, once stated:

The thing that puts fighting heart into any military organization is its spirit, and the Marines have their share of this and more. Military men here and in other countries have always admired the spirit of the Marines, our pride in our Corps. With all modesty, I believe it to be our most outstanding quality — a factor which has contributed more than anything else to our long and honorable record.

This point was effectively brought home to me during World War II by one of my commanding officers, Major J.P. (Pete) Haines. As a fledgling Marine aviator, I had heard much about how great the Marine Corps was. Underlying that at the time was the fact that the combat record of the Corps in the Pacific, even that early in the war, was outstanding. One day I somewhat flippantly asked Pete, "Major, what makes the Marines the best?" I have never forgotten his reply. This usually jovial man suddenly became very serious. He said the Marines were the best not only because of their training but because of their unique pride and esprit de corps. His final words on the subject, which I still vividly recall some 45 years later, were, "Marine training makes a man more afraid of letting his fellow Marines or his country down than he is of getting hurt himself."

It is just this attitude — this courage, dedication, and selfless devotion to duty — which is embodied in the Marine Corps motto, "Semper Fidelis" — Always Faithful. I am confident that the Marine Corps, and Marine Corps aviation, will deliver on this vow no less in the future than it has in the past.

Happy 75th Anniversary, Marine Corps Aviation!

Senator John Glenn

The sensation most prevalent during carrier operations is exhilaration. You know you are doing something that few people are capable of doing, and you are betting your life on doing it right. The people on the deck are betting on you, too, putting themselves in harm's way because they trust your skill and judgment.

— an F/A-18 pilot

The F-18 has technology like the space shuttle, with a cockpit optimized for pilots. Most of what I need to see — whether it's an air-to-ground or air-to-air weapon — is on the head-up display (HUD). I can see all my readings on the glass in front of me. Any changes I need to make can be made right on the HOTAS — the hands on throttle and stick — without reaching behind me for some obscure button.

Hornets have explosive acceleration — their performance is unbelievable. The feel of the airplane when you strap it on is great. Computers run the flight controls, which means that no matter what you want to do, the response is immediate. The systems can appear intimidating because they're so numerous, but you don't have to be a computer specialist to be able to fly the plane. Performance margins are so large on the F-18 that it's hard to get yourself into trouble.

— an F/A-18 pilot

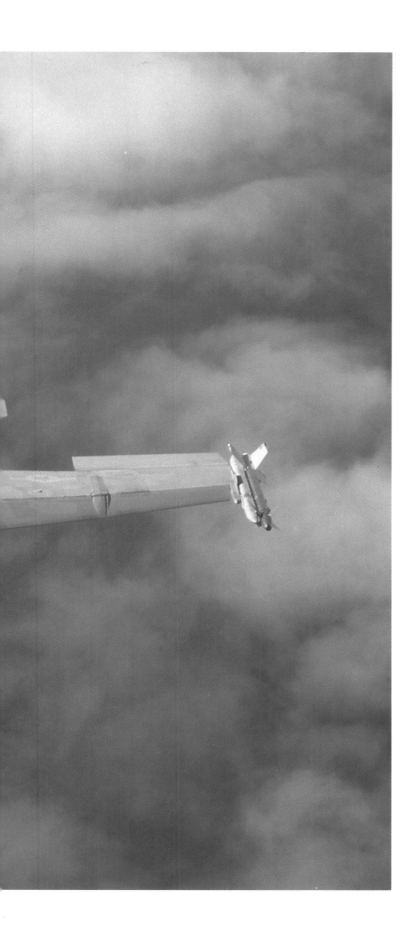

The problem most pilots have with the F-18 is loss of consciousness. Hornets can put on Gs so fast that the pilot can't prepare for it. Instead, pilots must be made aware of the power of their aircraft and trained to recognize the symptoms associated with too many Gs.

— an F/A-18 pilot

What makes a fighter pilot different from other aviators is that he is willing to bet his life against his adversary's life in aerial combat, winner take all. He must have good eyes and an ability to evaluate his adversary's energy and skill. It takes a "controlled aggressiveness" — an airborne discipline that he rarely subscribes to out of the cockpit.

— an F-18 pilot

The mission of the Cobra is to attack and to escort transports during the assault phase of an amphibious landing. With its sprint speed, it can react quickly in tactical situations. Once the amphibious objective has been achieved and the transports have received safe passage in and out of the beach area, the Cobra is assigned to a ground commander, who uses us for close-air support or tactical missions.

— an AH-1 pilot

A highly maneuverable aircraft, the Cobra is capable of a 60-degree angle of bank, which is quite good for a helicopter. They are quick to respond, which is why some people call them the "sports car" of helicopters.

The "Whiskey," the W model, is stronger than the T model because of its engine package and torque output. It also has a head-up display like fixed-wing aircraft. Altitude, heading, and other readings are superimposed on a glass panel in front of your face.

— an AH-1 pilot

At this time, we are converting most of the fleet over to a night-vision goggle system. These goggles, which flip up and down from the pilot's helmet, amplify available light at night. They do such a good job that we can launch on moonless nights with no trouble. Because enemy threat systems are so sophisticated, nighttime is becoming our best time to fly.

— an AH-1 pilot

For some, being assigned a tactical mission during the hours of darkness or during inclement weather causes concern. For Intruder crews, however, darkness and adverse weather are sources of security, because when visibility is reduced, so is the enemy threat. The enemy can run, but he can't hide. At night or during poor weather, he'll probably never know I was there — until it's too late to do anything about it.

— an A-6 bombardier/navigator

The best feature of the A-6 is its weapons system, one of the few all-weather weapons systems around. An A-6 pilot can bomb manually, but the computerized systems control the bombing for maximum accuracy.

I have a great deal of confidence in the Intruder's navigation systems, and its ground-mapping radar is among the finest in the world.

— an A-6 pilot

An A-6 Intruder may go out with a couple thousand pounds of bombs, drop them, and come back 2,000 pounds lighter. But in the EA-6 Prowler, we go out with 3,000 pounds of jamming pods, and we come back with 3,000 pounds of jamming pods, so we're just as heavy coming back aboard ship, which means we land at higher speeds. The weight also means fuel planning is more critical.

Given the high-tech nature of war, the Prowler has become popular. In the old days fighters had a saying, "If you move fast enough, you won't get hit." That is no longer true. Pilots just can't fly across their targets at 500 knots and expect to live.

— an EA-6 pilot

As the "ears" for the Marine Corps, the Prowler can fly into an area, plot out the enemy's defense network, and report that information back to the commander. From this information, a game plan is developed for hitting the target. EA-6B airplanes accompany the strikers when the game plan is carried out, protecting them by jamming enemy radars.

The Prowler grows on you. The first time I saw it, I thought it was the world's ugliest airplane. But after I flew it for a while, it began reminding me of the Heinz 57 mutt that I had as a kid. Pretty soon the Prowler was my favorite dog.

— an EA-6 pilot

The CH-53E Super Stallion is the assault pilot's dream machine. Smooth, responsive, and possessing maneuverability uncharacteristic for its size, it is a machine built for high-speed heavy lift. It routinely carries assault assets to amphibious assault forces — such as the 15,600-pound M-198 Howitzer or a 25,000-pound light-armored vehicle — at speeds in excess of 120 knots.

Super Stallions can also retrieve downed aircraft, a unique, heavy-lift capability.

— a CH-53E pilot

A two-point external lift is one where we have two pendants coming out of the helicopter. They are hooked to a load at two different points, a configuration that keeps the load stable. Heavier loads obviously have a tendency to pull on the aircraft, but even inexperienced pilots have little trouble. The load doesn't cause you to move around, because the helicopter still weighs more than what you are picking up.

— a CH-53E pilot

The Super Stallion is currently the only helicopter capable of aerial refueling. It's really no different than flying in formation, except that we're flying formation on the KC-130. The KC-130 provides a very stable platform, so it's not hard to hit the basket with the fuel probe. Of course, our rotors do come close to the tail of the tanker — about 50 feet away.

— a CH-53E pilot

With the Super Stallion's large rotor-diameter, we have to be careful when we land, but we still get into pretty small spots. We can work wherever other helicopters work as long as we're careful.

— a CH-53E pilot

The CH-53E performs extremely well on a carrier. Once we've landed, we fold our blades to the back, and the tail folds up around them. On deck there are tractors with towbars which hook on to the helicopter and drive it out of the way of other landing aircraft. Deck space on carriers is at a premium, so normally we only deploy four 53Es to each carrier.

— a CH-53E pilot

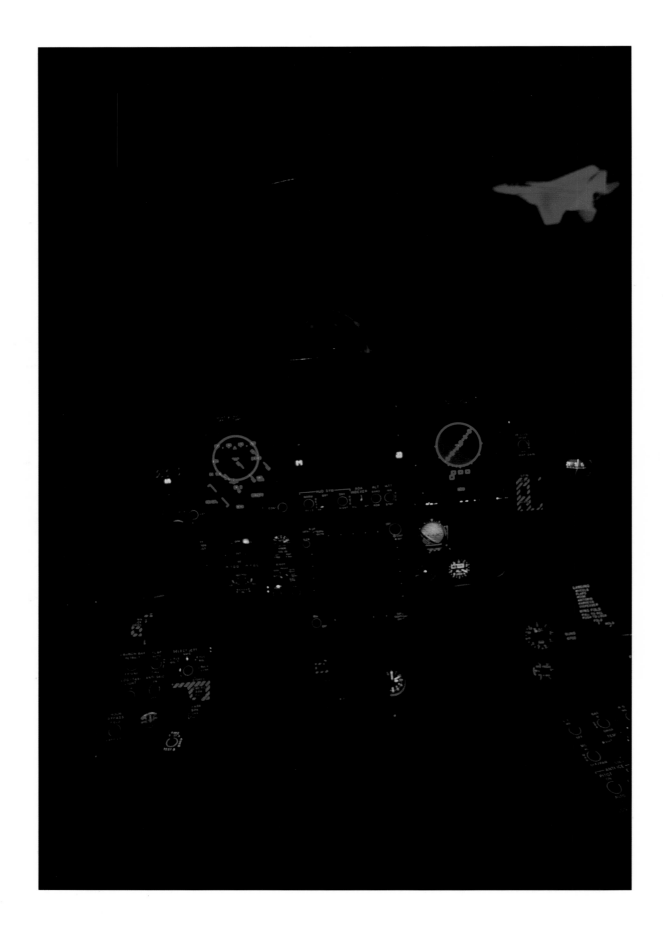

We have always had briefings before missions, where such things as objectives, frequencies being used, available fuel, emergency procedures, tactical issues, and other administrative details are discussed in full. Everything is covered, right down to planning for mishaps: What do you do if an airplane goes down? How do you call for a rescue helicopter? The goal is to be prepared for anything.

— a Marine Corps General

The Marine Corps relies on the A-4 Skyhawk for a variety of missions, including close-air support, deep-air support, and armed reconnaissance. It is also a lethal weapon in the air-to-air arena.

The most significant advancement in recent years for the A-4 is the Angular Rate Bombing System, a highly accurate system designed to reduce the pilot's work load in a high-threat environment. Its flight characteristics and bombing ability make it capable of carrying a multitude of ordnance, including nuclear weapons.

— an A-4 pilot

I really wanted to fly a single-seat airplane. To me, that was what flying was all about. You bring everything together yourself. Either you do the mission, or it doesn't get done.

When you strap on an A-4, the airplane becomes a part of you. Single-seat, single-engine aviation is something only few aviators experience these days. The A-4 is a pilot's airplane.

— an A-4 pilot

The Skyhawk is small, and it is easy to bang your head against the canopy of the plane just trying to unfold a map. In fact, we call the A-4 a "two-fold" airplane, because there is only enough room to open a map by two folds.

— an A-4 pilot

With 1960s technology, the F-4 has a number of idiosyncrasies. It will depart controlled flight more easily than new fighters, but the F-4 is a rugged, durable beast. Many flew in combat, sustained damage, and got their pilots back. Since it was not the best performing fighter, we learned to compensate to get performance out of it. It all depended on pilot effort. I have affection for the F-4 because it was hard to be good at flying it and because I flew it for seven years without it killing me.

— an F-4 pilot

Aerial refueling is the life's blood of an F-4, because fuel equals potential speed, and speed often means longer life. There is a sense of comfort knowing that a tanker is available, not only because you need the gasoline to return home, but because the more gas you get, the longer you can fly and fight.

— an F-4 pilot

The main mission of the KC-130 is aerial refueling. As a flying gas station, we ensure that other aircraft don't have to travel far from the battle to fill up. Our availability means that strikers can take off with less fuel in order to carry more ordnance into combat.

Another mission of the KC-130 is troop transport. In fact, we'll transport anything that supports a tactical mission, short of a tank. We can deliver paratroopers, equipment, whatever, by air.

— a KC-130 pilot

During aerial refueling, it is the KC-130 pilot's responsibility to fly the airplane steady, providing a stable platform for receivers that are plugging into a fuel hose at 20,000 feet. Routinely, we orbit on a track, which keeps us from burning a lot of fuel so that we give away almost all the fuel we take off with.

When a formation of KC-130s flies, the only communication that receivers have with the tanker to which they are assigned is by signal lights on the pods. An amber light means the tanker is ready to refuel, green indicates the fuel is flowing, and red tells the pilot that the flow of fuel has stopped.

— a KC-130 pilot

To assist the KC-130 on short-field takeoffs and unimproved-field takeoffs, a jet-assisted takeoff (JATO) system is added. The JATO bottles produce the power of a fifth engine, which greatly accelerates takeoff speed. This can be a big help in a tactical situation when you have a mountain to get over.

Since the KC-130 has turbo-prop engines instead of turbo-jet engines, it can go into dirt fields where normal turbine engines shouldn't go. The props also facilitate short landings or landings in sand. It's amazing how fast you can come in, touch down, and either be at a dead stop or slow enough to turn.

— a KC-130 pilot

Spy-rigging is the special insertion and retraction of reconnaisance teams from an area that does not have a landing zone. A rope with loops on the end of it is lowered to a reconnaissance team on the ground. While the helicopter hovers above them, the team takes the rope and hooks harnesses to it. When they've finished, the helicopter accelerates, picking them up. They dangle from the rope until the pilot finds a place to let them back down.

— a CH-46 pilot

CH-46s are the backbone of our Marine Corps troop-lift capability. We usually work off ships since most of our missions are amphibious. In any combat situation you have to set up advance naval bases in order to support incoming troops. You need ports for ship-to-shore movements. Our job is to go in and help pave the way.

As medium-lift helicopters, CH-46s are unique. They can perform a lot of missions assigned to small utility helicopters and some of the missions that the large CH-53s are tasked to do. A tandem-rotor helicopter, the CH-46 hovers well, even in crosswinds. It is not as dependent on the direction of the wind for hovering as are most helicopters. It is also ideal for over-the-water, search-and-rescue, hoisting operations, because it doesn't produce much rotor downwash.

— a CH-46 pilot

The CH-46 has a winch that can be used in two ways. Internally, the winch is used for loading cargo. It pulls cargo up into the aircraft on cargo rails. Externally, the winch hangs from the center of the aircraft through a hatch. Some CH-46s have a boom hoist by the back door that swings out to the side for rescue operations.

— a CH-46 pilot

A pinnacle approach is made when the landing zone is too small for the helicopter. The pilot can set the two back wheels down on the edge of a cliff or the top of a rise and hover. Since the back of the aircraft has a rear loading ramp, he can then unload his troops or whatever cargo he has inside.

— a CH-46 pilot

As a utility helicopter, the Huey can take on any task. It can be fitted with guns, or it can serve as a medical-evacuation bird, troop transport, or cargo carrier. That's why I like the Huey. For a whole week I can do something different every day.

We primarily support the ground element. Anything they might want to do — parachute operations, rappelling, spy-rigging — we'll coordinate before we go out for flight. For safety we fly in sections of two, so that if one aircraft goes down, the other is able to assist in rescuing the crew.

— a UH-1 pilot

Our flight uniform comprises steel-toed safety boots, gloves, a fire-resistant flight suit, and an eight-pound safety vest, containing floatation gear, a survival kit, and a packet filled with medical supplies. We also carry a pocket radio, which oversteps all other frequencies in the event we need to call for help.

— a UH-1 pilot

What you get in the Marine air-ground team is a package, tailored to the type of situation you are going into. Each package, regardless of its size, has one commander, who oversees three major components: aviation combat, ground combat, and service support.

— an A-6 pilot

The Harrier can land almost anywhere. All it needs is a 72 × 72 pad. No other fixed-wing airplane can do that. It has so much power, it is like an engine with a saddle on it, and it hovers better than a helicopter.

They introduced us to the AV-8A by having us do vertical takeoffs. We simply centered the thing on a pad at Cherry Point and tried to run through our minds all the procedures and sequences they had taught us. I took a deep breath, pushed the throttle, and waited for something to happen. I didn't wait long. The airplane staggered — or jumped, depending on your perspective — into the air.

An instructor guided me by radio, helping me get the plane under control. He had me maneuver it around to get a feel for it. Finally, he tried to convince me that it was time to land. I felt a little like a pioneer in a new frontier.

— an AV-8B pilot

Two things set the Marines apart from other branches of the armed services: One, we're the only outfit with ground troops and an air force in the same service. Two, we have the Harrier.

The Harrier provides the ground commander with close-air support under a much wider variety of battlefield conditions than most conventional airplanes. It also does it quicker. That's what the Harrier is all about — getting to a location fast enough to save lives or win a battle.

— an AV-8B pilot

If you want to stay out of trouble in a Harrier, there are certain laws of VSTOL aerodynamics to which you must adhere. When you start to disregard these principles, when you don't listen to what other pilots have to say about the airplane, when you quit paying attention to what the aircraft is trying to tell you, then you're going to get into trouble.

It takes about six months of training to fly the Harrier. There is a boat syllabus, a couple of syllabuses on carrier falls and low-level navigations, an air-to-air gunnery syllabus, and an extensive formation syllabus. We also make two flights in the CH-46 to get the feel of an aircraft sitting still above the ground.

— an AV-8B pilot

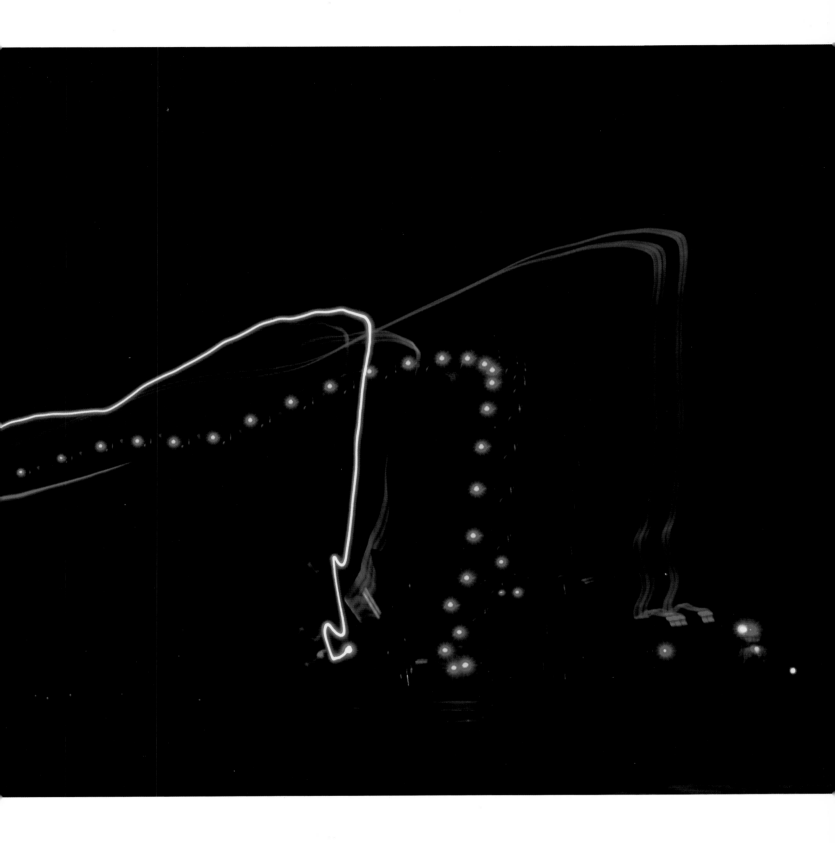

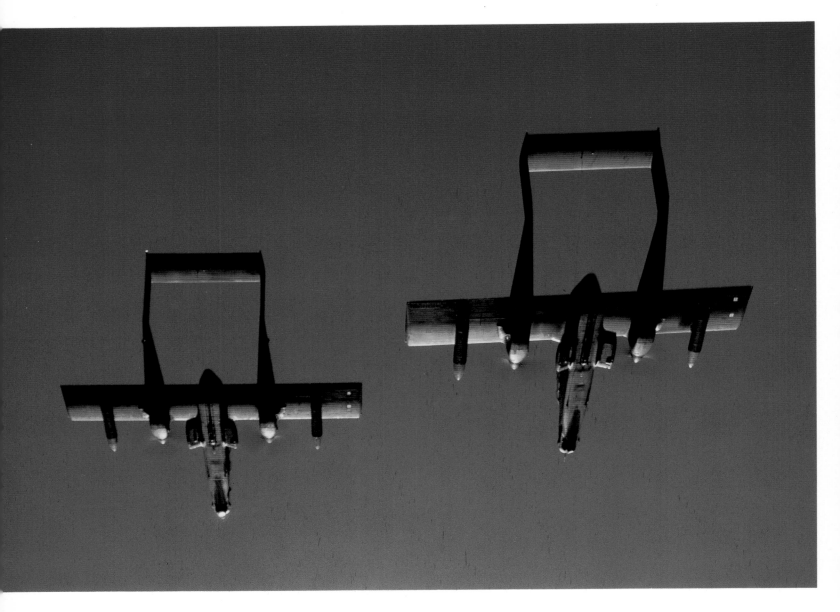

It doesn't roar through the skies at high speed, and it isn't the prettiest aircraft in the inventory, but the OV-10 Bronco is probably the most versatile. Reconnaissance, bomber, fighter, transport, medical evacuation — you name it, the Bronco can do it. Flying the OV-10 is sheer pleasure. It is intense, exciting low-level flying, where you can enjoy watching the terrain go by.

Ground officers fly on the OV-10 as aerial observers, taking their expertise and understanding of the events on the ground with them. Responsible for navigating, the aerial observers keep pilots informed about the terrain ahead.

Locating a loft point, firing the marking rocket, and guiding other aircraft onto the target while the plane flies at low altitude creates an intense working environment. If you can't be a pilot, being an aerial observer in the OV-10 Bronco has to be the next best thing.

— an OV-10 aerial observer

The OV-10 was built as a jungle fighter. It was designed to get in and out of small airfields, carry a lot of ordnance, and stay airborne for long periods. It is also capable of flying on just one engine, a procedure we practice often. An extremely maneuverable aircraft, the OV-10 flies well at slow speeds. Its STOL — short takeoff and landing — capabilities mean that it can take off like an elevator.

— an OV-10 pilot

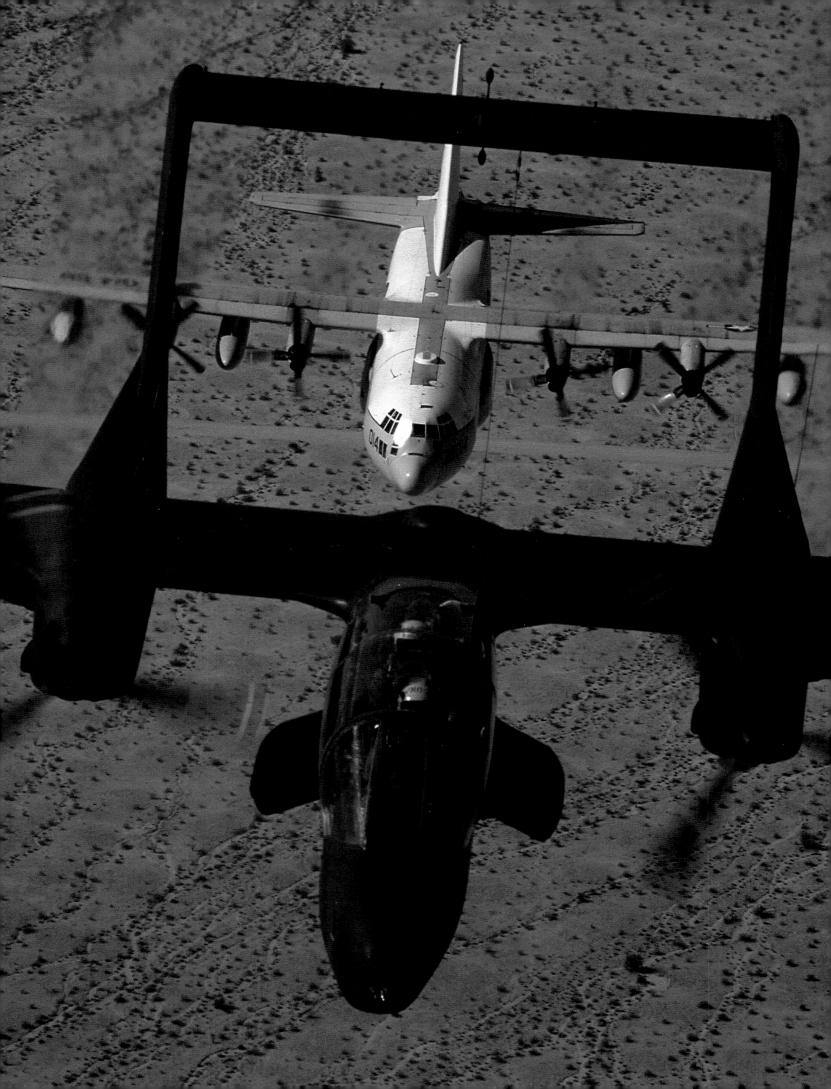

All but two of the color photographs in this book were made with Nikon 35mm cameras and Nikkor lenses, using Fujichrome 50, 100, and 400 film for color transparencies. Externally mounted pods and remotely controlled cameras were not used, because I wanted to put the reader inside the cockpit of each aircraft. Only then can you appreciate the incredible working environment of today's Marine aviator.

To protect my equipment from vibration, dust, and flying debris during helo operations, lens caps and skylight filters were necessary precautions. We operated day and night in all weather conditions. I was already familiar with the jet world, but there was more to learn about helicopters. Flying with 60 other aircraft below the horizon on a moonless night is intense and exhilarating. Helicopter pilots and crews are extremely tough. On a single mission temperatures inside the aircraft range from below freezing to above 100 degrees. It's a gritty, grimy, noisy business that does not have the glamour of the sleek, but sterile, jet community.

The Marine Corps' two prop planes, the KC-130 Hercules and the OV-10 Bronco, reminded me of the early days of aviation. With today's aviation technology, there is a tendency to view props as something old, not state-of-the-art. But the fact is that without these two capable, multi-mission aircraft, modern helo and jet communities could not operate on the battlefield.

And no Marine aviator would operate were it not for something else. While this is a book about aviation, it must be remembered that the only reason there are Marine aircraft is to support the Marine on the ground.

The following pages give a sampling of this proud, 75-year-old Marine Corps tradition.

— C.J. "Heater" Heatley, III

Roy S. Geiger (third from right and at controls of aircraft) became the fifth Marine Corps aviator in 1917 and went on to command squadrons in France, Haiti, and Nicaragua. Later he was commanding officer for all aviation units on Guadalcanal from September-November, 1942.

The original...aviation pioneers were regarded as harebrained

zealots by their fellow officers afloat and ashore, for there were very

few of the latter who believed that the flying machine was here to stay.

—John A. De Chant, DEVILBIRDS: THE STORY OF UNITED STATES

MARINE CORPS AVIATION IN WORLD WAR II

The First Aviation Squadron and the First Marine Aeronautic Company were formed on October 12, 1917, after the outbreak of WWI. After a year of training with British and French aviators, the first all-Marine raid occurred along the coast of Belgium in an attack of German submarine bases.

Douglas C-1 biplane receives routine maintenance in New York.

Commissioned by the Marine Corps in 1909, Alfred Cunningham received permission from his superiors to bring an airplane he had rented for $25 to the Philadelphia Navy Yard. The plane was so loud, Cunningham's colleagues dubbed it "Noisy Nan." The lieutenant tried everything from rebuilding the engine to constructing a ramp on the runway, hoping that the momentum achieved by bouncing up into the air would encourage "Nan" to stay aloft, but the plane wouldn't fly. Nevertheless, he attended the Naval Aviation Camp at Annapolis in 1912, becoming the first U.S. Marine Corps aviator.

USMC Private Cooper going up for a parachute jump.

Marines tighten the propeller of an aircraft at Parris Island, South Carolina.

An amphibious plane in Haiti, where Marines were stationed as early as 1915 to restore order in the politically and financially troubled country.

Sharing the perils and thrills of flying biplanes with their Army and Navy comrades,

Marine pilots had the added advantage of actual combat operations in Haiti, the Dominican

Republic, and Nicaragua, which they used to develop techniques for supporting ground troops.

Among those techniques was dive-bombing, first attempted by Lieutenant L.H.M. Sanderson

in 1919, which may be a unique Marine contribution to aerial warfare.

— Allan R. Millett, SEMPER FIDELIS: THE HISTORY

OF THE UNITED STATES MARINE CORPS

USMC aviator Francis T. Evans was the first person to master the flat spin and the first to loop a seaplane. His accomplishments earned him the Distinguished Flying Cross on June 10, 1936, nine months after the decoration was created.

The Marine Corps' first rotary-wing aircraft, the Pitcairn OP-1 autogyro, was field tested in Nicaragua in 1932. Unable to carry more than 200 pounds safely, the OP-1 was soon dropped from the USMC inventory.

BG-1 Great Lakes bomber plane.

Gunnery Sergeant Benjamin Belcher and Sergeant Jiggs, mascot, in Vought training plane at Quantico.

In all the far-flung combat zones of the Pacific, mascots made their way into the lives of Marines....Many pets were given rank,... service record books and uniforms and they were promoted or "busted" as their actions warranted.

—As told by Staff Sergeant William
Ross, SEMPER FIDELIS: THE U.S.
MARINES IN THE PACIFIC—1942-1945.

F3F-1s flying in wedge formation.

F3F-2 piloted by Captain C.A. Roberts.

Brewster F2A2 Buffalo, designed primarily for carrier operations, over Miami.

Grumman J2F-5 Duck at Quantico.

Corsairs move up the flight deck for a raid over the Truk Islands.

Vought F4U-1 Corsair lands on a Navy carrier following a strike against the Japanese.

Deck hands aboard the USS <u>Puget Sound</u> push a F6F Hellcat fighter into position for takeoff.

A lot of luck went into becoming an Ace pilot. Those of us fortunate enough to be senior pilots and in command were usually up front in formation, so we would get first crack at the enemy. Sometimes you might go out on a mission and not run into any enemy aircraft; another time you might go out and run into a poorly trained enemy formation and shoot down two or three airplanes. Then again, you might run into an enemy formation of veteran pilots who were as skillful as you.

— a Marine Corps general

Armed Curtiss SB2Cs from the "Bombing Banshees" squadron over Mindanao, the Philippine Islands. The turtle back on the plane in the background is collapsed to permit free use of the twin .30-caliber guns.

In 1847 an anonymous Marine on duty in Mexico wrote lyrics to be sung to a melody from a French operetta by Jacques Offenbach. The words and tune were later adopted as the official Marine Corps hymn. Although additional stanzas were added in 1929, the most significant change to the song occurred in 1942, when the line, "We fight our country's battles/On the land as on the sea," became, "We fight our country's battles/In the air, on land and sea," formally acknowledging the Marine Corps aviation arm.

Conditions on Guadalcanal did not allow much rest or relaxation. The pilots were living under exactly the same conditions as the other fighting marines. In the evenings they did their best to forget the war. There was a lot of kidding. They listened to a few well worn phonograph records, and played cards. Their only luxuries were a few bars of candy and cartons of American cigarettes delivered to them by dive-bombers from a nearby carrier.

—Keith Ayling, SEMPER FIDELIS:
THE U.S. MARINES IN ACTION

Aircraft from the first "Flying Nightmares" squadron on their way to take out Japanese installations between Rapopo and Tobera airfields, ten miles southeast of Raboul.

One wartime measure that temporarily broke the salt-encrusted hearts of the "Old Corps" was the enlistment of women Marines. A Women's Reserve of 18,000 to relieve men for combat duty was begun in February, 1943. That...was acceptable to the old hands in Aviation, but the thought of doing military duty side by side with "them glammer girls" was beyond belief—until they saw the dungareed WR's tear down a Corsair engine, or slide out, greased and grimed, from under a six-by-six truck, or handle a fouled-up air traffic pattern from a control tower with...ease....

—John A. De Chant, DEVILBIRDS: THE STORY OF UNITED STATES MARINE CORPS AVIATION IN WORLD WAR II

Accompanied by a fighter escort, Douglas R4D Skytrains carry casualties across the Pacific to a base hospital.

Kingfisher catapults from the USS <u>Texas</u>, Mediterranean Sea.

The first catapult takeoff from a battleship deck was attempted in 1915 by the Marine Corps' first aviator, Alfred Cunningham. During takeoff, the tail of the aircraft was damaged, so the plane stalled, turned over, and fell to the deck, breaking Cunningham's back. In 1916 he returned to active duty.

Guam's typhoon season, rivaling the Aleutians for foul flying weather, caught a night-fighter pilot in a rain squall. Radioed to come in by the Orote Field tower, Lieutenant Malcolm G. Moncrief... nosed down for a landing. The night was black. Pressure areas buffeted his Hellcat. Rain pounded on his windshield. He came in low over what he thought was the field and circled. He wasn't sure. He couldn't see much of anything. It was almost as black below as above.

The control tower men, hearing him twice come in and then zoom up again, called anxiously, "What's wrong? Can't you see the field?"

"Field, hell!" cracked back the exasperated pilot. "Where's Guam?"

—As told by Technical Sergeant
Peter B. Germano in SEMPER FIDELIS:
THE U.S. MARINES IN THE PACIFIC—
1942-1945

F4U Corsair fires its rockets into a Japanese stronghold on Okinawa.

Marine bombers flying from dirt airfields on Pacific islands caused serious damage to Japanese carriers during WWII.

Mechanics at a Marine base in the South Pacific lift the tail of a Corsair in order to align its machine guns.

Until the arrival of the Corsair fighter in February, 1943, the Wildcat was the mainstay of the air defense of Guadalcanal. It took an almost mechanically impossible punishment in the air and on the ground and kept on flying. It has been rightly said that if any single weapon saved Guadalcanal, it was this Grumman fighter. It became such a symbol to those on the ground that they resented for a while the arrival of the Corsair.

—John A. De Chant, DEVILBIRDS: THE STORY OF UNITED STATES
MARINE CORPS AVIATION IN WORLD WAR II

Crew members of a TBF torpedo dive-bomber put a "Tommy" gun aboard in the event of a forced landing in enemy territory.

The infantrymen, watching the daily air battles overhead from their foxholes, agreed that those "stick-jockies" really had it. By night, the pilots listened to the unholy noises of night battle along the perimeter and swore they had it easy and that the foot soldiers were the boys who did the work. And so as the melting pot at Guadalcanal simmered out the dross and the dead, each day the mutual respect of the air and ground teams increased for one another.

—John A. De Chant, DEVILBIRDS: THE STORY OF UNITED STATES MARINE CORPS AVIATION IN WORLD WAR II

Grumman TBF-1s flying in echelon formation.

Marine torpedo bombers taxi to runway on Bougainville, the Solomon Islands, for a sortie against enemy shipping lanes.

Long arguments were provoked by...what name to give to the much-shelled strategic road that ran along the island's perimeter. One of the most popular suggestions was "Seaview Boulevard." The debate never was settled to anyone's satisfaction. But long after the last shots were fired on Iwo Jima, most Marines who fought there found it hard to refer to it as anything but "that damned road."

—As told by Technical Sergeant Charles B. Cunningham
in SEMPER FIDELIS: THE U.S. MARINES IN THE PACIFIC—1942-1945

Corsair drops a bomb on enemy positions in "Bloody Nose Ridge," Palau Islands.

F4F Wildcat and crew.

The first Marine to hit the beach at Bougainville stumbled in the heavy surf, recovered and charged ashore. That first Marine is a man to meet, but our acquaintanceship was merely in passing. He had no time to look at me that hot November morning, and though I was looking hard for him, the glimpse was only fleeting. But I know I saw him. At least I saw a speck and a sliver of steel waver slightly in the haze of burning powder hanging over Empress Augusta Bay.

The first Marine was going his way, a few hard feet at a time, through the wet sand. I was going mine, snugly, riding at two hundred miles an hour in an Avenger bomber. We met there on the beach at Bougainville for, perhaps, a thousandth of a second. My watch said 7:23.

Someday I may get to shake the hand of that first Marine. He is a man to cultivate.

—As told by Captain Penn T. Kimball in SEMPER FIDELIS:

THE U.S. MARINES IN THE PACIFIC—1942-1945

F9F Panthers prepare for takeoff

On June 25, 1950, eight divisions of the North Korean People's Army crossed over the 38th parallel, beginning their campaign to unify the country as one communist state. While there was heated debate by armed services brass about whether to use air support against anything but enemy communication lines, Marine Corps officials insisted that their air and ground teams be sent to Korea as a package.

Corsair pilot from the "Polka Dot" squadron in Korea angles his approach so that the plane's arresting hook will catch the wire.

F7F-3N Tiger Cat night fighters ensured that aerial pressure was brought to bear against the enemy in Korea 24 hours a day.

Ground crewmen of the "Death Rattlers" fighter-bomber squadrons in Korea gather for a picture after their efforts enabled pilots to fly a record-breaking 2,887 hours and 819 combat sorties in a one-month period.

The mission of the Marine Corps is primarily offensive.

Any other role deprives us of our effectiveness.

—Holland McTyeire Smith, CORAL AND BRASS

Sikorsky HRS-1 hovers over rough terrain, dropping troops and cargo by rope and winch.

Troop transport helicopters on the flight deck of an aircraft carrier.

Wounded marines are loaded onto HTL-4s for transportation to medical units.

The helicopter was a tremendous development. It can evacuate an area of wounded and carry the injured to a first-aid station or field hospital in minutes. Helicopters carried troops into combat for the first time in Korea.

Division command post the day after Christmas in the Yongji-ri region of Korea.

I used to get a little worried before a mission, but once I got up in the air, I was working too hard to worry anymore. It was all business then. It's sort of like butterflies before a game. Once you're called in to play, you just perform.

— a Marine Corps pilot

FJ-4s in formation.

F2H Banshee.

Radar bombing was used for the first time in Korea. Also introduced during that war was the F2H-2P Banshee which gave photo-reconnaissance capabilities to the Marine Corps.

Marine aviation is special because it comes as a package. We have an air/ground team. We can go anyplace with the capability to conduct modern warfare with our ground units and aviation units fully integrated.

— a Marine Corps pilot

On July 16, 1957, USMC aviator John H. Glenn, Jr., flew the first North American, supersonic, transcontinental flight non-stop from NAS Los Alamitos, California, to NAS Floyd Bennett, New York, in an F8U Crusader.

Disabled A-4E Skyhawk is carried by CH-53A Sea Stallion to Da Nang, Vietnam. Lifting downed aircraft is a capability unique to CH-53s.

My first mission was what we called a "Tally-Ho," which entailed flying an A-6 at night in Vietnam to look for enemy trucks. In those days, the best way to hit a truck was with rockets. The enemy would shoot back at you, but their aim was poor because they shot at the sound, so these runs became like training flights for us.

— an A-6 pilot

Mobile arresting-equipment, which permits short-airfield landings, stops A-6A Intruder on its return from a bombing run in Vietnam.

Formation of KC-130s refuels F-4 Phantoms over the Johnson Islands during trans-Pacific flight to Vietnam.

Changes in aviation since WWII are unbelievable. The airplanes keep getting faster and faster. So many of today's planes are automated — everything is computerized. That doesn't mean a pilot shouldn't be highly skilled, though, or have a will to live, and possess keen flying instincts. Automation on today's planes actually gives the pilot more time to concentrate on the job at hand.

— a Marine Corps pilot

CH-46 Sea Knight prepares to refuel from the LST Westchester County in the Binh Son River, Vietnam.

The aircraft best remembered by American ground troops during Vietnam was the helicopter, which served in gunship, transport, and evacuation roles.

During "Operation Upshur Stream," a CH-46 helicopter drops supplies to "K" Company.

If I haven't seen a guy for 15 years, I may not remember his name, but I'll still remember him by his call sign. Living together, training together, and sharing risks make you close to the other men. It's like being on a football team where you play in the Superbowl every day.

— a Marine Corps pilot

UH-1E gunship fires rockets during a search-and-destroy mission.

Plane captains wash A-4E Skyhawks to prevent corrosion and clogging of moving parts.

With wings folded and chute billowing in the jet exhaust, a F-4J Phantom taxis back to its flight line after a mission.

We were told that there were MIGs nearby, so all the A-6s got airborne. We were assigned to fly low, with two fighters flying right behind us. The high force of the strike was to arrive about 30 seconds after we did.

When we entered the corridor, I saw one bogie, then two bogies. There were bogies all over the place — MIGs, 17s and 21s, flying on top of us.

We started bombing the target. The MIGs began dropping their tanks, hoping the tanks would hit us. Then all those MIGs began rolling in on us. By this time, the high force had arrived and was trying to pick them off our tails.

One 17 kept shooting at us. He made five passes, but he never hit us because we broke every time. Meanwhile, one of our guys flying a Phantom got behind the 17, but he couldn't fire until we got out of the way. He began screaming at us to break...the MIGs kept rolling in...we kept trying to work some angles to get out of his way...all these things were happening at once.

The Phantom pilot finally fired his rockets and blew the tail right off that 17.

— an A-6 pilot

CH-53 hovers after delivering cargo to a fire-support base 29 miles southwest of Da Nang.

Marines from Company "C," First Reconnaissance Battalion, ride in CH-46 helicopter to their insertion point.

Helicopter from HMM-263 drops Marine riflemen onto a sand bar at dawn on the second day of "Operation Orange," Vietnam.

Discipline is no less a fundamental plank

in the Marine platform than is preparedness.

— Albertus W. Catlin, WITH THE HELP

OF GOD AND A FEW MARINES

C-130 Hercules delivers supplies by parachute to Marines at the Khe Sanh combat base.

Sea Knights clear the runway at Marble Mountain and head toward An Hoa, Vietnam, on an assault against enemy forces.

CH-46 is marooned after being downed by enemy fire during flood evacuation mission in Vietnam.

The Marines are probably the oldest body of fighting men in the world. Both the Greeks and Romans had marine corps, known as the Epibatai and Charsiarii. They were described as land soldiers trained for sea service and were rowed or sailed to their points of action. Upon landing, they opened up the engagement to prepare the way for the main body of soldiers and artillery. Through the ages, all countries have developed their marines as advance shock troops. The phrase, ''The Marines have landed,'' is as old as the history of war.

— Keith Ayling, SEMPER FIDELIS: THE U.S. MARINES IN ACTION

Marines help wounded buddies to helicopter near Dong Ha after heavy fighting.

It is incumbent upon all of us in Marine aviation to prepare ourselves, both physically and mentally, for the possibility that this time out of the chocks, circumstances may call upon us to lay it all on the line.

— a Marine Corps pilot

A-4 SKYHAWK

Developed early in the 1950s, the A-4 Skyhawk is a lightweight, nuclear-strike-capability aircraft used in large numbers from aircraft carriers.

A light-attack, single-engine, jet aircraft, the Skyhawk was designed to destroy surface targets in support of the landing force commander, to escort helicopters, or to conduct other operations as directed.

There are numerous models of the A-4 in use. The A-4E/F/M and the OA-4M/TA-4F are currently used by Marine Corps active and reserve squadrons. All models are capable of delivering conventional and nuclear weapons under day and night Visual Meteorological Conditions. The A-4M uses a head-up display and computer-aided delivery of ordnance with the angle rate bombing system.

Manufacturer: Douglas Aircraft Company **Crew:** one pilot **Engine:** one Pratt & Whitney J52-P-408A turbojet, 11,200 pounds of thrust **Dimensions:** wingspan 27 feet 6 inches, length 41 feet 4 inches, height 15 feet **Weight:** 10,465 pounds (empty), 24,500 or 26,500 pounds (loaded) depending on model **Speed:** 670 mph clean at sea level (maximum), 645 mph (with 4,000 pounds of weapons) **Climb:** 8,440 feet per minute **Ceiling:** 42,250 feet **Range:** 2,055 nautical miles (maximum), 335 nautical miles (with 4,000 pounds of weapons) **Armament:** two 20mm Mk-12 cannons (200 rounds each) and either 14 500-pound bombs, three 1,000-pound bombs, one 2,000-pound bomb, four Shrike air-to-surface missiles, three Walleye air-to-surface missiles, four Laser Mavericks, or one Mk-28/43/57 nuclear weapon

Photographs: pages 12, 82, 83, 84, 85, 86-87, 88, 89

A-6 INTRUDER

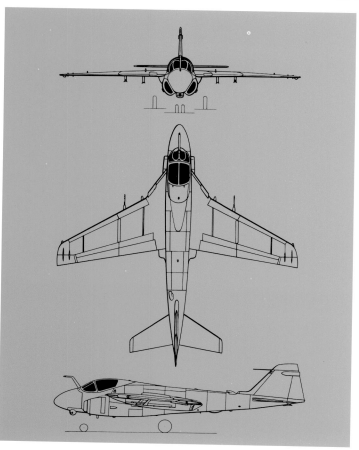

The A-6 Intruder, an all-weather, night-attack aircraft developed for conventional ground attack, was selected from 11 competing designs in December 1957.

In spite of its considerable weight, the Intruder has excellent slow-flying capabilities with full-span slats and flaps. It incorporates comprehensive navigation, radar, and attack systems. Sitting side-by-side, the crew has a view in all directions through a broad, sliding canopy.

The A-6E, the model currently in service, is being fitted with Target Recognition Attack Multisensors (TRAMs), a turreted electro-optical/infrared system matched with laser-guided weapons.

Manufacturer: Grumman Aerospace USA **Crew:** one pilot, one bombardier/navigator **Engine:** two Pratt & Whitney J-52 P-8 A/B two-shaft turbojets, each with 9,300 pounds of thrust **Dimensions:** wingspan 53 feet, length 54 feet 7 inches, height 16 feet 3 inches **Weight:** 25,630 pounds (empty), 60,626 pounds (loaded) **Speed:** 648 mph at sea level (maximum) **Climb:** 8,600 feet per minute **Ceiling:** 44,600 feet **Range:** 1,077 miles (with full combat load), 3,100 miles (with external fuel tanks) **Armament:** 30 500-pound bombs, or ten 1,000-pound bombs, or five 2,000-pound bombs, or three Mk-28/43/57 nuclear weapons

Photographs: pages 2-3, 12, 48, 48-49, 50, 50-51, 52-53, 54-55, 56-57, 58, 59

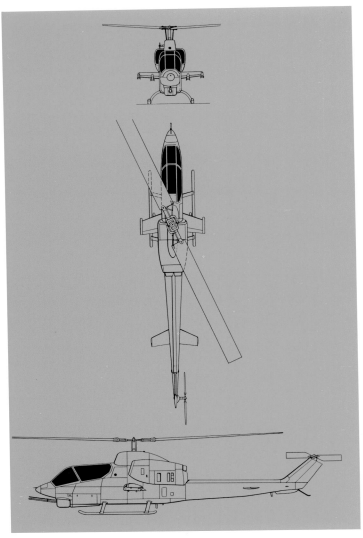

AH-1 COBRA

Following only six months of development, the Cobra made its first flight in 1965. The AH-1J Sea Cobra, with its narrow, 38-inch fuselage and stub wings, is capable of mounting rocket packs or gun pods and a nose-gun turret.

A two-seat, twin-engine, single-rotor, attack helicopter, the AH-1T is an improved version of the AH-1J, incorporating more powerful engines, a strengthened transmission, and greater ordnance capability.

Able to mount a TOW (Tube-launched, Optically-tracked, Wire-guided) missile system, the 1T also has anti-armor capability. Its two-stage, solid-propellant, command-guidance missiles attain speeds of more than 1,000 feet per second in the first one-and-one-half seconds of flight before coasting to the target.

Manufacturer: Bell Helicopter Textron USA **Crew:** one pilot, one gunner **Engine:** two United Aircraft of Canada T-400-CP-400 turboshafts, 1,800shp each **Dimensions:** main rotor diameter 44 feet, fuselage length 44 feet 7 inches, overall length 53 feet 4 inches, height 13 feet 8 inches **Weight:** 6,816 pounds (loaded), 10,000 pounds (maximum) **Speed:** 207 mph **Ceiling:** 10,550 feet, 9,900 feet (hovering in ground effect) **Range:** 360 nautical miles **Armament:** one 20mm XM-197 and either four XM-159 rocket packs (19 2.75-inch rockets per pack) or two 7.62mm XM-18E1 mini-gun pods

Photographs: pages 8-9, 36-37, 37, 38-39, 40-41, 42, 43, 44-45, 45, 46-47, 114-115, 132-133, 134-135

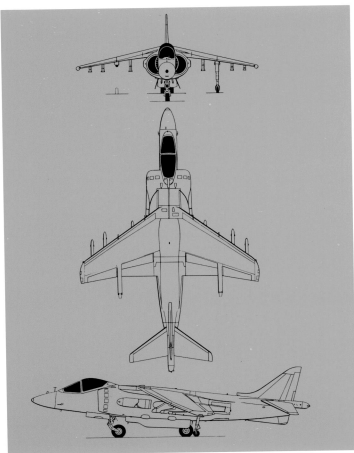

AV-8B HARRIER

Developed by the British, the Harrier was the first Vertical/Short Take-Off-and-Landing (V/STOL) aircraft to enter service with the U.S. armed forces. It employs a vectored-thrust engine which gives it V/STOL capability for use from Confined Area Landing Sites (CAL-Sites), ship pads, and small clearings ashore.

The AV-8A variant is a single-seat, tactical-attack aircraft adopted in 1969 by the Marine Corps for use in close air-support missions and air-defense roles. The AV-8B, an improved V/STOL version, includes a super-critical wing shape, larger trailing-edge flaps, drooped ailerons, strakes under the gun pods, redesigned engine intakes, and strengthened landing gear.

Despite a decision to improve aerodynamics at the expense of upgrading engine performance, the AV-8B excels the AV-8A in payload and range.

Manufacturer: McDonnell Douglas Corporation **Engine:** one Rolls-Royce Pegasus F402-RR-404 vectored-thrust turbofan, 21,500 pounds of thrust **Dimensions:** wingspan 30 feet 3 inches, length 46 feet 3 inches, height 11 feet 7 inches **Weight:** 12,550 pounds (empty), 29,750 pounds (maximum for short take-off), 18,850 pounds (maximum for vertical take-off) **Speed:** 650 mph (0.95 Mach) **Ceiling:** 50,000+ feet **Range:** 100-nautical-mile radius (with 7,800 pounds of weapons, vertical-take-off mode), 150-nautical-mile radius (with 6,000 pounds of weapons, short-take-off mode), 650-nautical-mile radius (with 3,500 pounds of weapons, short-take-off mode, no loiter time) **Armament:** two Sidewinder air-to-air missiles, and one 25mm Gatling gun with either 14 500-pound bombs, six 1,000-pound bombs, or four Maverick air-to-surface missiles

Photographs: pages 12, 76-77, 118-119, 136-137, 138, 139, 140-141, 142, 143, 144, 144-145, 146-147

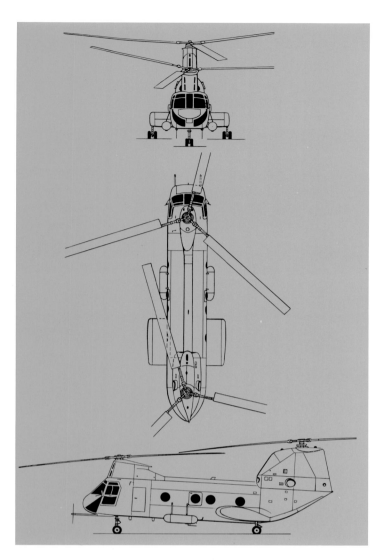

CH-46 SEA KNIGHT

Principal assault helicopter for the Marine Corps, the CH-46 Sea Knight provides helicopter transport of personnel for the landing force during ship-to-shore movements. Its secondary purpose is transporting equipment and supplies and providing search and rescue services.

Manufacturer: Boeing Vertol **Crew:** two pilots, one crewman **Engine:** two GE T58-GE-10 turboshafts, 1,400shp each **Dimensions:** main rotor diameter 51 feet, fuselage length 44 feet 10 inches, overall length 84 feet 4 inches, height 16 feet 8 inches **Weight:** 12,112 pounds (empty), 23,000 pounds (maximum) **Speed:** 166 mph, 140 mph (cruise) **Ceiling:** 14,000 feet, 9,500 feet (hovering in ground effect) **Range:** 206 nautical miles, 774 nautical miles (ferry range with external tanks) **Armament:** CH-46D/F — two 7.62mm M-60 machine guns or two .50-caliber M-2 machine guns **Payload:** 17 troops, or 15 litter patients and two attendants, or 4,200 pounds of cargo

Photographs: pages 70-71, 114-115, 115, 118-119, 121, 122, 122-123, 124-125, 132-133, 134-135

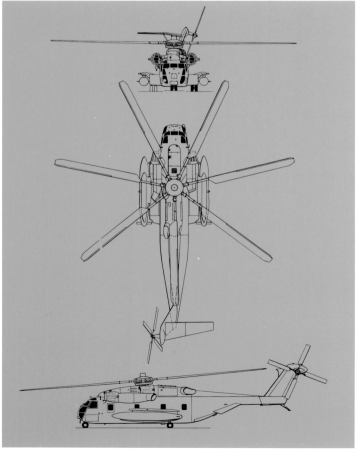

CH-53E SUPER STALLION

Using three engines, the CH-53E Super Stallion can lift 93 percent of all the heavy equipment in a Marine Division — including all Navy and Marine Corps fighter, attack, and electronic-warfare aircraft — compared to the 38 percent that can be hoisted by the CH-53D.

Super Stallions differ from other CH-53 variants because of their third engine, seven-blade main rotors, larger rotor blades, improved transmissions, in-flight fueling probes, provisions for 650-gallon fuel tanks on both landing gear sponsons, and different tail configurations.

Manufacturer: Sikorsky Aircraft, a Division of United Technologies USA **Crew:** two pilots, one crewman **Engine:** three GE T64-GE-416 turboshafts, 4,380shp each **Dimensions:** main rotor diameter 79 feet, fuselage length 91 feet 7 inches, overall length 99 feet 6 inches, height 28 feet 8 inches **Weight:** 33,826 pounds (empty), 70,000+ pounds (maximum) **Speed:** 196 mph **Range:** 50-nautical-mile radius (32,000 pounds of cargo), 500-nautical-mile radius (16,000 pounds of cargo), 1,000 nautical miles (ferry range) **Armament:** none **Payload:** 56 troops or 32,000 pounds of cargo

Photographs: pages 64-65, 66, 67, 68-69, 70-71, 72-73, 73, 74-75, 75, 76, 76-77, 78-79, 114-115, 118-119

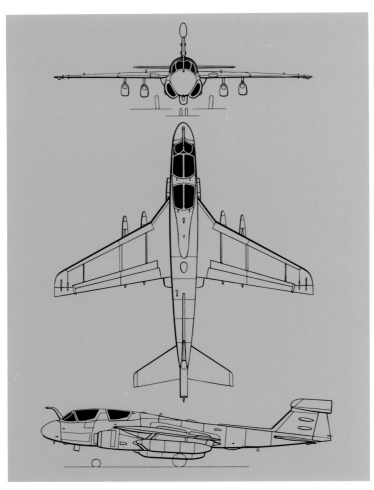

EA-6B PROWLER

With a history similar to that of the A-6 Intruder, the EA-6B Prowler is a totally redesigned, four-seat aircraft. Deployable from shore bases or aircraft carriers, the Prowler's payload comprises the most advanced and comprehensive electronic-countermeasures (ECM) equipment ever fitted to a tactical aircraft.

Its ALQ-99 Tactical Jamming System consists of onboard receivers and up to five externally mounted ECM pods, which contain windmill generators to supply electric power. The EA-6B is capable of providing ECM and tactical-intelligence support for Marine Air-Ground Task Force operations.

The EA-6B Prowler differs from the EA-6A in that the 6B has two additional systems operators and more sophisticated jamming equipment.

Manufacturer: Grumman Aerospace USA **Crew:** one pilot, three electronic systems operators **Engines:** two Pratt & Whitney J-52 P-408 turbojets, each with 11,200 pounds of thrust **Dimensions:** wingspan 53 feet, length 59 feet 5 inches, height 16 feet 3 inches **Weight:** 34,581 pounds (empty), 58,500 pounds (loaded) **Speed:** 660 mph at sea level (maximum), 477 mph (cruise) **Ceiling:** 39,000 feet **Range:** 710-nautical-mile radius (with four ECM pods) **Armament:** none **Payload:** five ALQ-99 jamming pods

Photographs: pages 12, 58, 60-61, 62-63, 98-99

F-4 PHANTOM

An all-weather, multi-purpose fighter, the F-4 Phantom has been in operation since the early 1960s.

Designed to intercept and destroy enemy aircraft and missiles in all types of weather and to attack and destroy surface targets in support of landing forces, the F-4J is fitted with an AWG-10A missile control system. This missile system includes the APG-59 radar, an ALE-29 chaff/infrared decoy dispenser, an ALQ-100A jamming system, an ALR-45F threat-warning receiver, and an APR-43 missile launch warning system. The F-4S is equipped with the improved ALQ-126 jamming system.

Production on the F-4 Phantom ceased in 1979, and the Marine Corps is replacing its F-4 inventory with the F/A-18 Hornet.

Manufacturer: McDonnell Douglas Corporation **Crew:** one pilot, one radar-intercept officer **Engine:** two GE J79-GE-10 turbojets, each with 17,900 pounds of thrust (with afterburner) **Dimensions:** wingspan 38 feet 5 inches, length 58 feet 3 inches, height 16 feet 3 inches **Weight:** 32,500 pounds (empty), 46,000 pounds (loaded clean), 56,000 pounds (maximum) **Speed:** 1,450 mph clean at 36,000 feet (Mach 2.1) **Ceiling:** 50,000 feet **Range:** 300-nautical-mile radius (with eight AAMs and six 500-pound bombs), 400-nautical-mile radius (with eight 500-pound bombs), 2,300 miles (ferry range) **Armament:** four Sparrow air-to-air missiles with either four Sidewinder air-to-air missiles, 24 250-pound bombs, or four Sidewinder air-to-air missiles and six 500-pound bombs

Photographs: 10-11, 12, 19, 90-91, 92-93, 94-95, 96-97, 98-99, 100-101

F/A-18 HORNET

The F/A-18 Hornet, which is currently replacing the F-4 Phantom, is a lightweight fighter/attack aircraft designed for carrier operations. A twin-engine, single-piloted, supersonic aircraft compatible with the full range of air-to-air and air-to-ground ordnance, the Hornet is agile and responsive.

The F/A-18 incorporates state-of-the-art technology, such as digital fly-by-wire flight controls, a multimode radar, and lightweight composites which enhance combat capabilities and the aircraft's flexibility. It also makes use of threat-warning and electronic countermeasures equipment.

Manufacturer: McDonnell Douglas Corporation **Crew:** one pilot **Engine:** two GE F404-GE-400 turbofans, each with 16,000 pounds of thrust **Dimensions:** wingspan 37 feet 6 inches, length 56 feet, height 15 feet 4 inches **Weight:** 33,585 pounds (loaded in fighter role), 47,000 pounds (loaded in attack role) **Speed:** Mach 1.8 **Ceiling:** 50,000 feet **Range:** 550-nautical-mile radius (with bombs or air-to-surface missiles) **Armament:** one 20mm M61A1 rotary-barrel gun (570 rounds) and either six Sidewinder air-to-air missiles and two Sparrow air-to-air missiles (fighter role) or two Sidewinder air-to-air missiles and 17,000 pounds of bombs/missiles (attack role)

Photographs: pages 4, 12, 22-23, 24, 25, 26-27, 28, 29, 30-31, 31, 32-33, 34, 35

KC-130 HERCULES

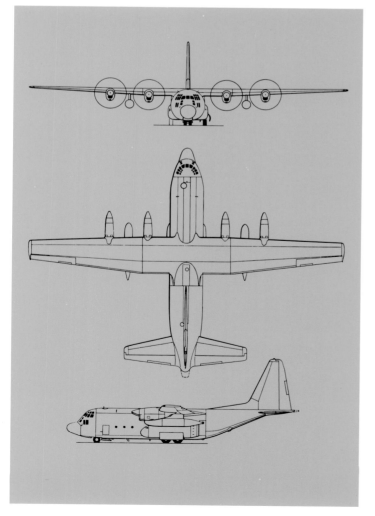

KC-130 aircraft are assigned to each Marine Corps Wing. Specific missions include in-flight refueling of tactical aircraft; air delivery of combat cargo and emergency supplies, including air drop between supply bases and small combat fields; inter-theater, aerial transport of personnel, equipment, and supplies; and long-range, direct delivery of high-priority material and personnel in emergency combat situations.

Manufacturer: Lockheed-Georgia Company USA **Crew:** two pilots, one navigator, one flight engineer, one radio operator/loadmaster **Engine:** four Allison T56-A-15 turboprops, 4,591shp each (maximum, T/O only), 4,061shp each (continuous) **Dimensions:** wingspan 132 feet 7 inches, length 99 feet 5 inches, height 38 feet 3 inches **Weight:** 75,368 pounds (empty), 109,744 pounds (loaded), 155,000 pounds (maximum), 175,000 pounds (maximum overload) **Speed:** 348 mph at 19,000 feet, 331 mph (cruise) **Ceiling:** 25,000 feet **Range:** 2,564-nautical-mile radius (maximum payload); 3,734-nautical-mile radius (maximum fuel); 1,000-nautical-mile radius (tanker missions with 32,140 pounds of fuel transferred) **Armament:** none **Payload:** 92 troops, or 64 paratroopers, or 26,913 pounds of cargo

Photographs: 10-11, 17, 59, 100-101, 101, 102-103, 104, 105, 106-107, 107, 108, 109, 110-111, 112-113, 154, 158-159

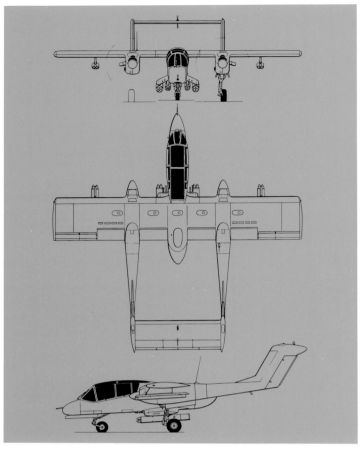

OV-10 BRONCO

The Bronco is a multi-purpose, light-attack aircraft flown by two Marine observation squadrons to conduct visual aerial reconnaissance missions. They provide transportation for aerial radiological reconnaissance, tactical air observation, artillery and naval-gunfire spotting, and airborne control of tactical air-support operations.

Other tasks performed by the OV-10 include armed escort for helicopters and limited, front-line, low-level aerial photography. The Bronco can be used for short take-off and landings on aircraft carriers without the use of catapults.

By removing the second seat, the OV-10 Bronco is able to carry 3,200 pounds of cargo, five paratroopers, or two litter patients and an attendant.

Manufacturer: Rockwell International **Crew:** one pilot, one observer
Engine: two Garrett Research T76-G-10/10A/12/12A turboprops, 715shp each
Dimensions: wingspan 40 feet, length 41 feet 7 inches, height 15 feet 2 inches
Weight: 6,969 pounds (empty), 9,908 pounds (loaded), 14,466 pounds (maximum)
Speed: 281 mph clean at sea level **Range:** 228-nautical-mile radius (attack role), 1,430 nautical miles (ferry range) **Armament:** four 7.62mm machine guns, bombs, rocket pods, and fuel tanks on five wing-and-fuselage stations

Photographs: pages 6-7, 16, 148-149, 150, 151, 152, 153, 154, 155, 156-157, 158-159, 160

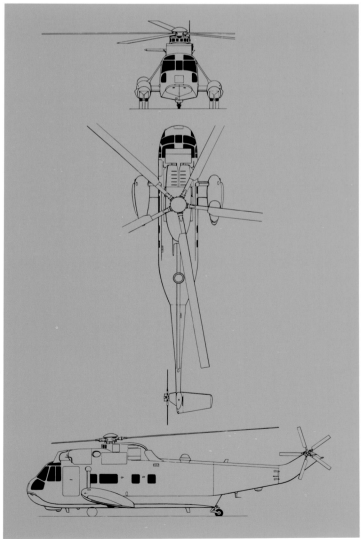

S-61

Produced by Sikorsky Aircraft, the S-61 is the generic model of several popular helicopters. Two commercial versions are the S-61N and the S-61L, both of which use the major mechanical components of the twin-turbine-powered SH-3 antisubmarine-warfare helicopters produced by Sikorsky for the U.S. Navy. The S-61N, which has sponsons for water landings, is used around the world for offshore oil transportation missions. The S-61L has conventional fixed landing gear.

Another helicopter based on the Navy's SH-3 model is the VH-3D Sea King. Used only by Marine helicopter squadron HMX-1, known as ''Marine One,'' the VH-3D provides safe, efficient transportation for the President of the United States. It is equipped with a special communications package, enabling the President to contact any part of the world in an instant.

S-61s have flown more passengers more miles than any other helicopter in the world, and they have flown more than three times as many hours in instrument weather as all other commercial helicopters combined.

Manufacturer: Sikorsky Aircraft, a Division of United Technologies USA
Crew: two pilots, two crewmen **Engine:** two GE CT-58-140-2 turboshafts, 1,500shp each **Dimensions:** main rotor diameter 62 feet, fuselage length 59 feet 4 inches, overall length 72 feet 10 inches, height 17 feet 5 inches
Weight: 20,500 pounds **Speed:** 150 mph (maximum), 140 mph (cruise) **Ceiling:** 12,500 feet **Range:** 282 miles **Armament:** none **Payload:** 30-35 passengers

Photograph: page 14 (VH-3D)

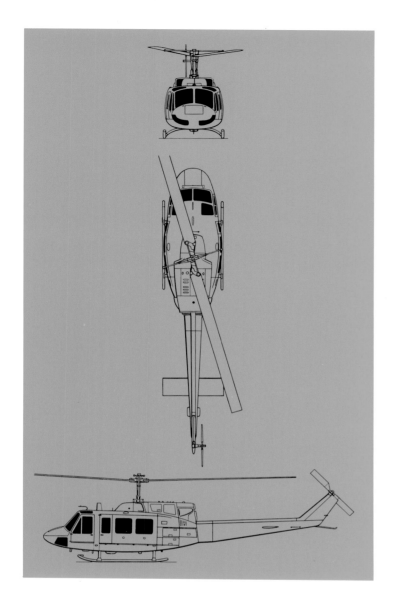

UH-1N HUEY

With more than 9,000 produced from the 1950s to the present, the Huey is considered to be the most widely used helicopter in the world, being flown today by about 40 nations. Its primary mission is to provide utility combat-helicopter support to the landing force in ship-to-shore movements and in subsequent operations ashore.

The UH-1N, which has space for six litter patients and one medical attendant, can also be used as a primary medical evacuation aircraft. An external cargo suspension unit provides the 1N with external cargo capability.

Manufacturer: Bell Helicopter Textron USA **Crew:** one pilot **Engine:** two United Aircraft of Canada PT6 turboshafts, 900shp each **Dimensions:** main rotor diameter 48 feet 2 inches, fuselage length 45 feet 5 inches, overall length 57 feet 3 inches, height 14 feet 5 inches **Weight:** 5,549 pounds (empty), 10,500 pounds (maximum) **Speed:** 126 mph **Ceiling:** 15,000 feet, 12,900 feet (hovering in ground effect) **Range:** 250 nautical miles **Armament:** 7.62mm M-60 machine guns, or 7.62 GAU-2 B/A mini-guns, or a .50-caliber M-2 machine gun, or 2.75-inch rocket pods **Payload:** 16 troops, or combinations of troops, guns, and rockets

Photographs: pages 114-115, 126, 127, 128, 129, 130-131

Special thanks to Lieutenant Colonel Fred "Assassin" McCorkle and the War Eagles of MAWTS-1 and to Lieutenant Colonel Don "Groucho" Persky, Commanding Officer of VMO-2.

The publisher gratefully acknowledges the assistance of Lieutenant Colonel John M. Shotwell, Phillip P. Upschulte, and the people of the United States Marine Corps.